SACRAMENTS
IN MY
REFRIGERATOR

SACRAMENTS
IN MY
REFRIGERATOR

by
Mary Sue H. Rosenberger

The Brethren Press. Elgin, Illinois

Library of Congress Cataloging in Publication Data

Rosenberger, Mary Sue, 1940—
"Sacraments in my refrigerator."

1. Prayers. 2. Meditations. I. Title.
BV245.R67   242'.8   79-502
ISBN O-87178-769-5

Published by **The Brethren Press, Elgin, Illinois 60120**

Distributed by The Two Continents Publishing Group, LTD.
171 Madison Avenue, New York, New York 10016

Dedication

To the men in my life:
my husband Bruce, and
my sons Luke and Joel
who lovingly supply my refrigerator;
and to the memory of my father,
Russ Helstern,
who challenged me to look for sacraments.

CONTENTS

III. " . . . unto us a child is born . . . "

IV. " . . . treasure in clay vessels . . . "

Introduction

This is not a book of poetry; it is certainly not prose; and if the word "prayer" raises images in your mind of cathedrals and clerical incantations, it is not even a book of prayers! It is rather a diary of window-raising; an account of experiences which have opened windows in my life through which God's light and love could then shine into areas previously dark.

These little revelations have come out of very common situations in my life:

—personal wrestling with image or decisions
—the deep sharing of life and love with another person in marriage
—the fun and frustration of rearing two sons
—the everyday duties of housekeeping, gardening, etc.
—professional practice as a registered nurse in a nursing home, and
—the joys and disappointments of the church as seen from the perspective of a pastor's wife.

In the midst of experiences such as picking beans, family squabbles, church meetings and checking the pulse of a dying patient, I have often been brought to my spiritual knees by the wonder of how God communicates the divine to us in the commonplace. Hence the title chosen for this little book, "Sacraments in my Refrigerator," and its contents are meant to convey that mystery.

I pray that God might use something contained in this little book to open a window in your life through which He might shine more brightly than before.

Mary Sue H. Rosenberger

11

One Woman's Dilemma

Women's rights — women's duties!

Lord, I'm confused!
I'm a woman — —
 and that's about all I know for sure
 in this age of controversy
 over what that gender means!

"Equal pay for equal work"
 "No second class citizens"
 "Women, too, should have freedom of choice"
That all makes sense to me. But so does
 "A woman is the hub of her family and home"
 "The home is the best institution for education"
"Sacrifice for husband and family"

I've enjoyed my professional life —
 having my own money
 independence, dignity
 and the prestige of being a somebody in the world!
But there's fulfillment, too, in
 the smell of baking bread, and a meal of vegetables I tended
 and preserved
 the sight of two bright, happy children dressed in clothes
 I made myself
 the feel of a hug and a kiss that says
 "I'm somebody to at least one person!"
And the frustrations were always the same —
 too much to do
 too little time
 the fascinating foibles of people
 all magnified by my own lack of perfection.
And I can't blame them all on discrimination or housework!

Surely, Lord, there must be a middle ground for me
somewhere between The Total Woman and its
me-manipulation
and Woman's Awareness and its me-worship!

Those who spout liberation seem so bound they are right
And those settled in traditional roles seem equally bound all
others are wrong.
Myself, I've never found the answers to life's questions
to be quite that simple!

Lord, God, help me in my confusion!
Even your Word doesn't make it clear to me because
maybe there is "neither male nor female . . . in Christ
Jesus",
but women should keep their "heads covered" and their
mouths closed in church!

I don't presume to know what is Right and Wrong —
That, Lord, is your dominion —
and I couldn't manage such lofty knowledge, anyway!
Only help me to know where —
in the midst of this female-strom —
you want me to be
at this moment in time!

I.

"I, alone . . ."

Life-trak

As if on an express train
    You speed us through life,
      ticketed by time!

Through windows we catch dizzying,
    distant glimpses
      of people and places
      of grandeur and grime—
too far and too fast to feel
      to smell
      to know.

Occasional short pauses of celebration
    break in on us—
  But no stopping.
Congenial fellow-travellers come and go,
  but it is, after all,
    a solitary journey.
  One way—no going back.

We're glad to hurry through the dark tunnels
  and past the precipices
But couldn't we linger on the mountaintops
  or stop to touch a hand that waves
    as we rush by?

Only the knowledge of Your presence
    at the controls
  and Your hand on the throttle
Transforms our travel
    from prison to purpose.

Creating

Creator of All,

From resting in the hollow of Your hand,
You call me, the created to assist in Your
creative tasks—
having been loved, I am to love
having been fed, I am to feed
having been enriched, I am to enrich.

But, oh what a temptation
to sit back, relax, and let You do it!

Keep molding Your image on me—
try chiseling if necessary!

Used

I prayed to be used by You, Lord—
    not used up.

But, here I am,
    collapsed and weary
        from doing Your work.

I know all about that "mount up with wings
    as eagles" stuff
        and I'm grateful for those promises,
        they hold me together at a time like this.

So, I'm waiting—exhausted but expectant—
    for You to pour in the power
        for Your next task.

Meditation on the Evening Paper

God—I'm scared!
    Death screams from every line
        death for not being black—or white
            not American—or Asian
            not right—or wrong
        the too soon die and the too late
        the young and the old—DIE.

Here and thirty hours away by jet
    Communist and capitalist
    pauper and philanthrope
    author and aborigine—DIE
    and are buried side by side.

Oh, God—dying can be so quick these days,
    But it takes time to live and there's so little time left, for
    Crises are already upon us—
        nuclear war in minutes
        radiation death in hours
        death by tumor and smog statistically
        and the death of nothingness continuously.

Death is "not being"—but that is not the fear
    for I was not before I was.
But God, I scream, I want time "to be" before I am not again!

The answer comes, not from the newsprint,
    But in the echoes of my scream:
    "Being needs only *You* and *today*
    and living is but a series of well-used nows."

Praise God for now.
Hallelujah for chaos and challenge, today's beauty!
"For these, Thy gifts, Lord, make me truly thankful."

Too Tired to Pray

Lord, I'm just too tired to pray tonight!
    Everytime I close my eyes
        and search for words of meditation
    I'm overwhelmed by the vision
        of a soft, inviting bed!

But You who knew me before I was born
And who knows my word before it is on my lips,
    You know there was praise
        in my tasks of the day.
    And penitence in my tired, aching back.
    There was thanksgiving over clean clothes
      and tasty meals,
    Petition throughout eight hours
      of passing medications and changing dressings
    And, in my throbbing legs, confession
      of not having enough time
      for the really important things,
        like the smell of the lilacs
        and sitting with the dying.

Thank You for the freedom
      to pray with my hands and feet
      as well as words,
    But oh, how I need a quiet season of rest
        in You!

New Mother Identity Crisis

Lord, God,
    What do I have to call my own?
        my energy is taken by my infant son,
        my independence is shared with my husband,
        and my time is consumed by the dish-pan, washer and
            the
            vacuum cleaner!

    But should I need anything beyond
        a healthy son,
        a loving husband,
        and an orderly house?

Yes, Lord,
    I need to learn the joy of giving—
            not begrudging—
        for I need to be needed,
    and I need to learn that I am more than a body
        and a span of time!

Hard Labor

My God—

    Sometimes it's hard work to pray!
        When the burden on my shoulders
            seems too heavy
        When the fog in my mind
            seems too thick
        When my distance from Your presence
            seems too great
    Then—when I need You most—
            praying seems like work
            and I can only groan in my distress.

But You knew distress, too,
    at Gethsemane and Calvary
    and can accept my groans and tears
        as well as my Thees and Thous.
        Thank You.

Proof

Faith proven true
    is no longer faith—
            but fact,
    and moves from the realm
        of challenge and cheer
            to concrete!

But, oh, how I'd like to know—
        for sure!

"Lord, help Thou my unbelief!"

Comfort Station

Today I'm a nobody
    knowing nothing
        doing nothing right
            and taking it out on everybody around me!

God—
    May I crawl into Your lap, please,
        and cry myself back into perspective again?

Snap-Back

Lord, I feel like a rubber-band!
   Stretched to my capacity
      by this pressing problem
      and that crushing concern
   Pulled this way and that
      by conflicting ideas
      and differing glimpses of truth.

Grant me the extra flexibility of Your grace
   that I might not snap—
      but snap back again to the center
      of my being—in Yourself.

Grace

Home, free, by faith
Acceptance by accepting
Freedom from fear
        by fixating—
    on the will of God!

Oh my God,
    What a relief!

Aging

Designer of Life,
    What good planning it is
    that You've put old age
    at the end of life
        not at the beginning
        or the middle.

    You've given us time to prepare;
        To gather the wisdom
            and maturity
        needed to contend with
            the aches of age.

    Thank you.

II.

" . . . two shall become one . . . "

Connubial Classroom

Love Divine and Original,
    In the black of night
    I stretch out my hand
        and touch a hand
        which I find already extended to me.
With fingers intertwined
    I can unwind, rest,
        and become, again, human by sharing.

In the pinks and gold of daybreak
I stretch out my hand
    and touch a hand
    which was waiting for mine.
Through clasped fingers
    I sense excitement, opportunities
    and glimpse the divine in purpose.

Ah, how much we have learned of You—
        from each other in marriage.

Reflection

Source of Light and Love,
    I marvel at the mystery of human love,
       and wonder if it is not really
           only that
        which we have allowed
        You to plant and grow
          in our hearts,
        reflected back to us by the loved one
           as a mirror?

Real love must come from You,
    not from us
    nor from those around us,
Because polishing love's reflection in the beloved
      is such a poor excuse
      for our own lovelessness!

The Love Cake

Celestial Chef,

    On the day we were married,
        I thought to myself;
            "Today I have tasted
                what love really is!"

    But, after these few short years
        Spiced with laughter and children,
        Baked by troubles and frustrations,
    Now I know that on that day,
        I was really only licking the beaters!

    Thanks for the delicious lesson!

"What God Has Joined Together . . . "

Lord God—
    Is it because we take our covenant with
        You so lightly
    That we so readily break our covenants
        with each other?

    Covenants called
        loving,
            promises,
                marriage. . . .

Oh, God,
    Your Son died to free us from our sins,
        not our responsibilities.

Rat Race

God of Order and not Confusion—
    I feel like I'm running through life
    Galloping off frantically after one bright
             butterfly or another
And leaving my mate far away to go running
           after his own butterflies.

I miss having time together
    to study the clouds
    or savor the wildflowers along the path.

Surely You don't intend our life together
       to be such a breathless race—
    Or do You?
For, I understand that further down the path
You send fewer butterflies—and more wildflowers!

Life Filled Full

Women's meetings
Women searching
In knowledge and accomplishments
In child-bearing and mothering
In church and religion
For liberation? fulfillment? for meaning.

Thank You, God, that I can come home
    That's 'where it's at' for me.
Not that I search in my family—
    mine is no search, but a pilgrimage.
And not that I find my meaning in them—
    that I found myself before we were us.
But that we are fellow pilgrims together
Each pointing out lodestars, guideposts
      and the fragrance of roadside violets.
Each enriching our paths toward You—
      by sharing.

How free and full a life I have 'like it is.'

III.

"... unto us
a child
is born ..."

Anxiously Awaiting

It's good to feel a child move inside my body,
How warm to be loved both inside and out.

But I fear for this child, Father—
                did You for Yours?

This world is no fit place for a child
A polluted planet ready to begrime a helpless sunbeam
A boot to stamp out that shell-less creature.
Just look what it did to Your Son!

And mothers around the world share this fear, I think.
Not pot, free-love and affluence, perhaps,
But hunger, rats and American money!
And, since time began, mothers have worried:
            the Indians, grizzly bears and typhoid fever
            the king, debtors' prison and evil spirits,
            and always, hating, war and killing.

Was Mary fearful, too? and yet she sang:
        "My heart praises the Lord
        My soul is glad because of God . . . "

Familial Acrobatics

Heavenly Parent of us all,

Building a human family
seems so much like
building a human pyramid!
Stand firm here,
relax to balance there,
try to equalize the weight
but add extra strength
where the load gets heavy,
don't move suddenly, individually
or the whole structure
is in danger of
T
O
P
P
L
I
N
G
!
And, always, steady,
steady,
steady!

How much easier to build on the solid foundation
of Yourself
than on the empty space
of our own understanding!

But it still takes lots of balance,
lots of patience,
and enough love to hold it all together!

Mixed Blessings

Behold!
    If children are an inheritance of You, Lord
    Today I almost wish You had left me out
        of that will and testament!

    How can two little beings—
        not yet possessing a second-grade education
            between them—
        be at once so intelligent and so infuriating
            so loving—and so pig-headed
            so fascinating—and so frustrating!

    How can two little creatures—
        who together are less than 90 pounds—
        possess the power to drive their full-grown
            maternal parent
            to irrational behavior?
No doubt it's their talent to openly exhibit
        the sins of the fathers (and mothers), visited
            upon the second generation,
        Sins which we have not yet accepted in ourselves!

No, Lord, I don't really want retroactive
        birth control,
But I do wish You'd sent an instruction manual
        with Your inheritance,
        or some kind of a guarantee!

Trust and Teddy Bears

Heavenly Father,
    Like a child with his teddy bear,
        How we like to tuck You under our arms,
           like our own private security object—
           hugging You close when we're lonely,
           leaving You forgotten on the floor
                when we get engrossed in other amusements!

How can we ignore the reality
    that You created us
    and could, if You wanted to,
        drag us through life by an arm or a leg?
We can ignore it because You don't!
    Instead, You turn us loose from Your grasp
        and bid us stand on our own two feet before You.
        Then, You prop us up on a cross,
           and strengthen our floppy legs
               with Your spirit!

Ah, how much easier it is to play at being You
        than to stand before You!

Freedom

Like a toddler in a playpen, Lord
    How we cry for our freedom
        from restrictions around us;
            from family ties or boring work
            from limited time or finances
            from energy shortage or physical pain.

And, like that toddler, we cannot know
    That we clamor for the freedom
        to fall down the stairs
        to burn ourselves on the stove
        or to lose ourselves in an unfamiliar maze.

How grateful we are that you do not give us
        what we ask for
    But what we need.

Father, visit this tid-bit of wisdom upon this
        clamoring climber
    Before he deafens us all!

Religious Freedom

The Bill of Rights insures it
    and mother-love compels it
But I still have to bite my tongue sometimes,
      Lord,
      not to interrupt—
        with correction
          or chuckles—
      the sacred rite of the preschooler's
        bedtime prayers.

Surely with Your infinite wisdom
    and Your boundless love,
You can sort out the nursery rhymes,
      the riddles,
      and the nonsense,
      and accept his prayerful intentions
        without the help of my censorship!

Bedtime Prayers

"Please bless our family . . .
      Thank You God, Amen."

Every evening this sacred duty—
    hearing the bedtime prayers.

Help *me*, dear Lord, night after night, to see it—
    not as required routine to rush through
        or tune out
    nor as opportunity to spy out the secret sins
        of two little boys
        like some peeping St. Tom—
But, with proper respect and awe,
    to realize that in this rite,
        each eve I catch a fleeting glimpse
        inside two budding souls!
How I should tremble at that sight!

Dawdling

Lord—we have a problem at our house.
    A problem with time-tables—
        my sons's does not seem to be the same
        as mine!
    "Son, now it's time to eat—not play
        silly games."
    "Look, it's time to get undressed—
        we don't have all night, you know."

But, I must confess—
    You sometimes have the same problem with me!
    "Behold, now is the acceptable time,
      behold, this is the day of salvation"
        You tell me through St. Paul.
    And, yet, I go on filling my mind and my time
      with things other than
        Your Word
          and Your Will.
Please forgive my damnable dawdling!

First Day of School

He looks so little as he struggles up the high steps
    of the school bus!

Please, Lord, reach down and give him a boost—
    The first of many he'll need
        through the big steps and high climbs
        of future lessons in living!

Thanks, Lord, for being there to help when I can't be.

Sick Child

How I hover over one of the children
           when he's sick,
    Unwilling to let him out of my sight
        for a moment.
Unseen by his fever-clouded eyes,
     I watch,
        wait,
            and listen for his every request,
            praying for the moment those eyes will open,
            and I'll hear,
                "Gee, Mom, I feel better."

And You, who came to doctor sinners, not the
                righteous,
    You are like that, too, I think,
        hovering closer to us in our sin-sickness
        than in our goodness!
Unseen by our self-centered eyes,
     You watch,
        wait,
            and listen to our every request,
        hoping for the moment those eyes shall open
        to perceive Your presence
          and Your cure.

Fit for the Kingdom

"Except you become as a little child,
        you cannot enter the Kingdom of God."

Oh, Lord,—
        What bedlam You must have in Your domain!
                Gallons of spilled milk
                bushels of dirty diapers
                acres of muddy footprints
                        on celestial carpets
                the deafening din of a
                        community wrestling match
                and the squeals of "That's mine,
                        that's mine, that's all mine!"
You know, Lord—I'm not sure I want in.
        It sounds too much like home!

But, on the other hand,
        I guess You would also have
                time to play in the snow
                handfuls of freshly picked spring flowers
                thousands of sweaty hugs and
                        juicy kisses
                lots of honest smiles and un-neurotic tears
                and hundreds of hard questions, like:
                        "Why do we have so much food and so many
                                people are so hungry?"

On second thought, Lord,—
        Maybe it wouldn't be so bad after all!
        It sounds a lot like home.

If I repented of my "adultness"—
        and of the "adultness" I try to teach
                my children—
        Might there be a little spot in that Kingdom
                for me?

IV.

" . . . treasure in clay vessels . . . "

New Day

Morning comes like a birthday gift—
   an expected surprise!
And here it is, a day not yet opened
 not yet handled,
   or used
    or filled
     or wasted
      or marred
       or spent.

Great Giver of Time,
 What a challenge and responsibility
   wrapped in red and gold ribbons
   of sunrise.

Sacraments in My Refrigerator

It seems like blasphemy on Monday, Jesus,
To open the parsonage refrigerator and find
    Your symbolic Body and Blood
Stored away amidst my milk, eggs and left-over chicken gravy
Awaiting the partaking by shut-ins.

Only yesterday You were lifted up
    by silver tray and crystal goblet
    accompanied by prayers, vows and incantations
    holy, mysterious and unapproachable.

But, today, here you are, in the midst of my every-day
    boiled eggs and catsup.

And, Lord, I'm beginning to suspect you prefer it here,
    Because You loved the common folk of Galilee
        and
    Because You've hidden so much of Your truth in
        the common things of our lives.

Thank You for blessing my cottage cheese and carrots—
    as well as the assembled congregation.

Patterns

Creator of Life,
    In my handiwork I observe patterns
       of variety and color—
            now knit one, now purl two
            now increase, now decrease
            now gold, now black
    all combining to make the finished piece
       more beautiful and more useful.

    Could it be, in Your handiwork—my life—
       that the patterns I observe—
            now success, now failure
            now happiness, now discouragement
            now light, now dark
  are combining to make the finished piece
       more beautiful and more useful?
Then, thank you, Lord, for depression
          and struggle!

Tuned Out

Hey, God—where are You?
Have You tuned me out today?

In the din of the yelling, the foot-stamping
and the squash of the bowl of oatmeal
upside-down on the floor
Can't You hear my frustration
at my fractured schedule?
You're not listening to my disillusionment
at my interrupted ideas
Lord, You're ignoring my pleas
for Your presence and Your peace!
If You're really a God of order—
bring some into this chaos—NOW!

What's that, Still Small Voice?
"Who's tuned out to whom?"

Cold-snap

Fifteen degrees below zero!
      Brrrrr!
No wonder we call your love "warmth",
      Lord God!
      How miserable we are without it,
         —and how vulnerable.

      So we wrap ourselves—
         in Your absence—
      with layers and layers of things
      to convince ourselves we don't miss You.

      Please melt through our self-deception
         and warm our lives again!

Blizzard

Master of the Elements,
    To us who usually bask in Your blessings,
      surrounded by signs of Your love,
This sudden, relentless, unreasoning
      display of Your power is disturbing.

    The thin thread
      that binds us to life and sanity
        is twisted and tossed
          by the howling winds,
And, as You announce in the driving snow,
    "I am the Lord—and I am in control,"
      we nervously complain of interrupted schedules
          and broken-down conveniences!

Root us in Yourself instead of Your gifts
    that we might welcome Your chastisement
      as well as Your charity!

Flu

Yes, Lord,
    You do "move in a mysterious way,
        Your wonders to perform."
    You use the simple
        to shame the wise
    You use the common
        to convey the divine.
And now You have used a virus—
        too small to be seen—
to reduce my schedule to bedrest,
        to cloud my mind with
            the black fog of depression
      and leave me nothing
            but an aching, feverish, restless
            lump of lethargy!

And so I wait,
    resting in You,
        hoping that Your future wonders
        will include patience,
           healing power,
   and some suitable (nonviolent) revenge
        on that virus!

Alteration

Cut, hemmed, pressed and hung.
The drapes have been altered for new use.

Oh, Master of Change, who doesn't change—
    Would that my sinful self
        and my comfortable life
    Might be so readily altered
        from tradition and form
        to respond to the new needs
            and changing challenges
        through which you are calling in
            today's world.
    But fear, selfishness and apathy
        plague me like an empty bobbin
            and a knot in the thread.

Fill me and free me
    To be altered to your specifications.

Supermarket Survival

Consider the challenge of the supermarket
   Seemingly endless shelves of brightly
      packaged products
   from AlphaBits to Ziploc bags.
   A vast array—highly advertised and alluring
      good, bad, better, best.
   But, oh, the decisions demanded:
      Which to choose and which to ignore?
   And always the crowds shoving, the TV ads
      pushing and the nagging questions of
         finances and
            needs versus wants.

You know, Lord, my life's a bit like that, too.
   Seemingly endless bright opportunities
      from astrophysics to Zen-Buddhism
   A vast array—highly touted and tempting
      good, bad, better, best.
   But oh, the decisions demanded:
      Which to choose and which to ignore?
   And always the crowd shoving, the "me-want"
      pushing, and the nagging questions of
         time, talents and
            the will of God.

Creator of life and all its possibilities—
   Help me choose wisely and survive through
      this supermarket existence
   And keep reminding me that the store
      belongs to You!

Grace-Cycle

Now really, Lord,
   Just what is this *grace*
   You so freely bestow and
      we so unknowingly accept?

   I know it's the means to salvation,
      the vehicle to virtue and victory.
   But, tell me, what is it really like?

Is it a chauffered limosine—
   whisking us through our earthly journey
      in spite of ourselves?
      cushioning us from the rough spots,
      curtaining out the ugliness?
Or is it more like a bus—
   gathering us together on the same route
      for the same destination
   stopping and starting at the whim
      of any and all?
Or is Your grace like a bicycle—
   augmenting our own weak powers
      to speed us on life's journey
      leaving us vulnerable to the elements
         and the other traffic
      and requiring endurance, balance
         and a good sense of humor?

Frankly, Lord,
   If it's all the same to You,
   Just for the fun of it,
   I'll take the two-wheeled type!

City

As "nature abhors a vacuum"
    So, it seems to me, it must abhor a city!
        the traffic, the trample
        the concrete, the crowds
        the busyness, the buildings
        the noise, the neighbor-less-ness
    all unnatural—like a wound needing healing!

Creator of Village and Valley,
    Keep reminding this country girl
        that You love people!
    And, as cities are concentrations
        of those You love,
    Perhaps You love them the more!

Entertaining

Scrub, scour, dust, vacuum,
    cook, bake, straighten,—collapse.
There, all ready for company,
Except,
    Now my house is better prepared than my heart
    My table is prettier than my temperament
    Entertaining has become exhausting!

Lord,
    Calm my 'Martha-ness'
    With the joyous expectation
    That You will be among my guests tonight,
    And that You'll be seeking ME
        not a spotless house
        or a gourmet meal!

Kaleidoscopes

Despite our best human efforts
   at openness and acceptance
   at listening and loving
  we remain but
    kaleidoscopes
     to each other—
    bits of brightly-colored experiences
     reflected to view in another's mirrors.

 Small wonder we have
    misunderstandings,
     conflict,
      even war.

Great Knower of us all,
  polish our mirrors,
     fogged with self-interest,
    with Your grace,
      Your patience,
      Your love.

Tension or Truth

Good Giver of the Gift of Time,
    So caught up was I in a rat race
      of church duties

    That only reluctantly did I agree
      to take time for a
        family bike ride!
There I saw daffodils nodding in
    the brisk spring breeze
    a new spring colt
      a freshly plowed field
    a blush of green on the weeping willows
    a blue herron, awkward for a moment
      on its way to swooping grace
I heard a killdeer
      and a brook singing over its
        rocky bed
    the whir of the wheels
      and the bleat of a hungry lamb.
The wind was in my face, and
    as the tension drained away,
    I knew what You meant
      when Jesus said,
"God is a spirit, and they that worship Him
    must worship in spirit and in truth."

Weed-pulling

Lord,
    There's something therapeutic about pulling weeds,
        especially the big ones that smother the potato plants,
        and, of course, the thistles.
    It's as if, in partnership with You,
        I'm uprooting evil,
            exorcising the earth.

How I wish it were as easy to uproot
    the "weeds" from the
        garden of the world,
    especially the big ones that smother people
    and, of course, the spiny ones that hurt them.
But that's Your job, God,
    and I know that You've been pulling
        at them for centuries.
Let me help You where I can.

Lesson in a Loaf

It's only a loaf of bread, Lord
    But in my hand I see a doughy parable
        of my life in you.

I could have bought it, you see.
    For a modest sum—
        say a quarter or
            a buck in the offering plate—
    I could be feeding on someone else's experience.
But how tasteless and empty
    compared with loving it into existence myself
        the measuring and mixing
        the work and the worry
        the anticipation and the aroma
    and seeing with my own eyes,
        the transforming magic of the yeast!

Now, having been kneaded to fine texture and
    baked to a golden brown by a hot oven,
        the loaf gives itself to feed others.

But—Am *I* ready to be that loaf?

Building Blocks

Master Builder,
    Like a child building a block-tower,
    You have carefully—
            and complexly—
                    made us,
        painstakingly stacking
                one experience
                    on
                    top
                    of
                another.
Sometimes a heavy, new experience-block
    makes us totter,
                unstable,
        ready to fall!
But it was Your hand that placed it,
    and Your hand can steady!

Worship and the Bean Patch

Lord, what a lesson:
    You can't pick beans standing up!
    Try as I might,
        unless I bend my back or my knees
            I miss those long, green blessings
                hidden away amongst the leaves.

And worship is like that, too, I think.
    Try as we might,
        unless we bend our self-satisfied backs
        or our know-it-all knees
    we'll miss the blessings hidden away
            amongst the rituals!

Bicycling

Rhythmic exorcism of
     the evil spirits within.
   Lethargy leaks away
     in the throbbing
       of two hard-cranking legs.
   Tension trickles out
    at a tough
       ten miles an hour
        and
 Apathy is awakened to enjoyment
   by the rush of the wind
     the sound of a bird-song
       and the sight of a darting rabbit
        along the road.

Thank You, Lord, that the age of miracles is not past.
You *do* still drive out demons!

Oaks and Acorns

Creator of Time,
    I witness Your patience in the size of
        this great oak tree
and, slumped exhaustedly in its shade,
I realize with shame that my patience
        is not even the size of an acorn!

Can you lend me a little
    perspective,
        persistence and
            patience—right now—
    until mine grows?

Refining

That's it!
> That does it!
>> I've had it with her!
How ungrateful can she be—
> And after all I've done for her!

Oh, Jesus—
> Thank You, that through all those long years
>> when I turned my back on You,
> You never once said of me
>> what I've just said of her!
> Forgive me, please,
>> and, with the fire of Your Spirit,
>>> burn off that sediment of self-righteousness
>>> to purify Your presence in me.

Wings

Oh, for a pair of wings like that gull
To fly up and away
    high above the sea of doubt
        that is breaking over my soul
    and the mind-altering fatigue
        that weighs down my thoughts and steps.

But, wisely, Creator God,
    You've not given me wings for escape
        but arms which You've promised to strengthen
        and legs which shall not fail
          as I keep on keeping on.

Home-canned Theology

Great Author of All,
  How I admire the books of theology
    on the shelves of my husband's study
But my shelves hold a different type:
Your truths,
    picked from the garden of home and church
    blanched by my own experience and study
    then preserved under the pressure of daily life,
Mine is the home-canned variety!
It's not prepared for public consumption
    but it's tasty, easily digested
      and has proven to be nourishing!

Reunion

Father,
    Is heaven like a family reunion?
        tables loaded with bodily nourishment
        and spirits feasting on fellowship
            with loved ones not seen for awhile?

    Oh, I hope it is—
        I would much prefer that to golden streets
            and angel choirs!

Flight

"Welcome aboard Flight 77. We hope you
    have a pleasant trip."

Why is it, Heavenly Pilot,
    that we can, so readily and nonchalantly,
        trust ourselves and our mortality
        to an unseen pilot in the cockpit
and, so reluctantly or rebelliously, refuse
        to do the same with You,
            who made both plane and pilot
            who gave him knowledge and judgment
            and who holds us all in Your
                loving hands?

What illogical creatures we humans are!

Gulp

How much easier to repent initially of the sins of ignorance
Than daily of the sins of good-intention.

A one-time dose of the bitter tonic of pride
        can be eagerly swallowed
But as a daily diet
        it becomes difficult to choke down.

Perhaps what is needed, Lord, is a more frequent drink
        of cool, clear prayer!

Alarm!

God—
    Like a global alarm clock,
Our world rings a warning—
      in energy crises,
          starving children
               and in "wars and rumors of wars"—
Echoing Your words,
    "Woe to you who are rich . . . "

Can You wake us,
      sending us groping in the dark to respond?
Or, will we pull our
      "American way of life"
      over our heads—
    and go back to sleep?

Prayer of a Modern Day Publican

God—
    You've called so many people to accomplish great things
        saints to be victorious through suffering
        martyrs to be faithful to death
        preachers to be filled with your inspiration
        teachers to love the truth above all else
        doctors to heal the ills of the forgotten
        writers to move the consciences of many
        activists and peacemakers to free the enslaved
        parents to love with no limits or let-up.

And then there's me!

Dear God, the calls I hear sound so different—
        to fix a meal, to wash dishes
        to read to a tot, to wash diapers
        to puzzle through preparation for a Sunday school
            lesson
        to answer the phone and listen awhile
            (she really has problems!)
        to love my baby quiet after shouting didn't work
        through grumbles, to type a letter for my husband

Is it really Your voice, God?
    The same voice that calls others to greatness
        calling me to averageness?

Or—please forgive me, God—
    maybe I'm just hard-of-hearing!

Autumn

Master Painter,
As the days grow short
    and the chill winds blow
You color the trees more beautifully every day,
    brushing the leaves with brilliant hues
                of reds and golds until
      suddenly
        and quietly
            they fall.

And our lives should be like that, too,
           I think,
For, as the days grow short
    and the bones begin to chill,
You color our days with the brilliant hues
        of experience and wisdom,
But we—
      we miss the beauty and see only the fall,
For, by worshipping the fleeting youth of spring
    we have become blinded to the deep beauty of autumn!

Gift-wrapped

Ribbons and wrappings,
    scissors and tape!
Here I sit amidst my Christmas-challenge
    of concealing the contents
    of boxes and bundles
    as attractively as possible,
Knowing in my inner self
    that the best of surprises
    often come out of plain brown bags!

Great Giver of all Good—
    How like Christmas packages are we all!
    All year long, but especially at Christmas,
      we try to gift-wrap ourselves
      as attractively as possible
    Forgetting—in our primping
        and impression-making—
      that we cannot hide from You
      what You, Yourself, have given us!

    Please forgive us,
      for we know, in our inner selves,
      that the best of contents
      are usually stored in plain wrappings!

V.

" . . . sick and you cared . . . "

Rx

Some see You as Lord,
    some as Father or Mother
But I can see You, too, as Nurse
       tending
          comforting
             caring for us, sick as we are,
    with the terminal illness of SIN,
       offering to us the miracle cure—
         served up on a cross!

Often as not we refuse its bitter humiliation
    But You continue to tend
         to comfort
            to care
              to offer,
    as we kill ourselves with attempts
    at self-diagnosis
       and self-treatment!

Nursing Home

Oh, Jesus—
 Maybe You were fortunate
  to die at thirty-three!
 At seventy-three or eighty-three
  You, too, might have been confined
   and forgotten
   or dismissed as senile
   as are some of these around us here.

Comforter of the sick and lonely—
 Fill this place with Your love.
 And fill me with it, too,
  as I walk these halls in Your name.
 Fill my eyes so I will see
  the smiles and tears
  instead of wrinkles and stroke-sodden limbs
 Fill my ears so they will hear
  the feelings and music of souls
  instead of the babbling of senility
   or the fearful question in my own soul:
 "Will I be like this in thirty-five years?"

Life's journey of aging is a journey of faith—
 more rigorous than most of us realize—
 Fill me with faith—
  so that it flows from my fingertips
  to all those I touch today!

Condition: Poor

Irregular breathing
    unseeing eyes
        no response
            stillness.

Grieving family
    suffering relatives
        weeping loved ones
            questions.

Source of Life,
    Is it dying that's hard,
        or living?

Prisoners

She's a prisoner, Lord.
　　Just as surely as if confined by bars or chains,
　　　　eighty-five years,
　　　　　　illness
　　　　　　　　and circumstances
　　　　have imprisoned her.

And You said we are "to proclaim liberty
　　　　to the captives
　　　　and set free those who are oppressed,"
　　But tonight I feel more like a jailer
　　　　　　than a liberator,
　　　　because she's driving me *crazy!*
　　This is at least the twenty-fifth time
　　　　　I've answered her questions:
　　　　"Can I go home after supper?"
　　　　　"When can I go home?"
　　　　"Why can't I go home?"
　　　　　　"Where will I stay?"
　　　　"How can I pay to stay here?"
　　　　　　"Does my family know where I am?"
　　　　"When will they come to take me home?"
　　　　all asked in the shriek of deafness!

But, then, Lord,
　　Maybe the reason she bugs me
　　　　is because I feel imprisoned, too,
　　Confined by the clock,
　　　　routines, schedules,
　　　　　　expectations, demands,
　　　　　　　　fatigue,
　　　　　　habits and hopelessness.

Oh, Lord Jesus—
　　　　free us both!

Hospital

Great Healer,
>A baby was born today.
>His proud father passed out cigars and
>>bragged about his button nose
>>and his chances for the White House.

>A man was in pain today.
>His body was restless
>>but his cast-iron face held fast the tears.

>A family was happy today.
>Gallstones, the surgeon said,
>>not tumor, and health can be restored.

>A woman was lonely today.
>Her frightened cries were prayers
>>for a hand to hold
>>and an ear to listen.

>A mother died today.
>Her teen-aged daughters cried,
>>then prayed,
>>then went out into the rain.

>We see the scope of life
>>when we walk the halls of a hospital.
>We feel the depth of life
>>when we wait in its lobby or chapel.
>We know the meaning of life
>>When we study the faces of those being cared for
>>and those who care.

Forgive us for seeking that meaning in technological tamperings
>and ignoring Your power and presence.

"Vegetable" Gardening

Master of Life and Growth and Death,

> Here he lies—
> > still
> > > unseeing eyes
> > > > unable to move
> > > > > no response
> > > > > > but steady breathing.

In pity, contempt or just plain thoughtlessness,
some might call him a "vegetable".

But—
> even if he were—
> > he's growing in Your garden,
> > and it is on Your orders
> > > we feed
> > > > water
> > > > > and nurture.
> But, how often we'd like to forget that
> and choose for ourselves
> > when
> > > where
> > who
> > > > how much
> > > > > and how long to cultivate.

I'd rather tend "vegetables" in Your garden
than consume the fruits of self-indulgence!

Courage

Courage doesn't always wear khaki
        or stand before kings or courts
            giving witness in ringing tones.
Sometimes it sits all day in a chair—
            trapped by weakness
            wasting with disease—
        wearing a cherry smile
        and sharing an encouraging word!

Thank You, Redeemer, for the beauty
        of this brace and gentle soul
    and thank You for the place You've prepared for her
        —near the head of Your table, I think.

Coma

Where is she, Great Physician, what does she know?
Does she know the "now"?
    or is she trapped in the "then"?
In these last days, does she feel a gentle touch,
            or a hurried hand?
    or is she again part of the hurt or the happiness
            long past?

As You call her to Yourself,
        free her from all the anguish of then and now
        to the knowledge that she is loved.
Then help us be Your tools to make love real.

Cancer

Malignancy mocks our mortality,
　　making the present a fog
　　and the future a guessing game.

You who control the movement of the planets,
　　the change of seasons,
　　and the budding of a flower,
　Do You not also control the death-dealing division of cells?

Move us, in faith,
　　past the presumptous question, "Why?"
　　to accept that—
　　　　without consulting us—
　　　You *do* control.

VI.

" . . . the body of Christ . . . "

Sunday's Surgery

Worship exposes a deep nerve in us
Which, all through the work-a-day week,
    has been calloused with cares
        bruised by busyness
            overlooked in overwork.

But on Sunday, here it is,
    laid bare before You.
Sometimes You soothe us
    and sometimes disturb us.
But always You touch us
    awakening us to remember
    what it is like to be
        alive to the core—
           resurrected!

Priority Perch

If religion were the opiate of the people,
    Then, prayer would be an escape-hatch!
But, Lord, it's not.
Faith is not cop-out but contact
    with You who creates us in our chaos
        knows us in our ignorance
            directs us in our disintegration
        loves us in our selfishness
            and ultimately judges it all.
And prayer becomes, then,
            our priority perch—
                a high place, designed for
                    perspective,
                        approach to power
                and a refreshed return to the
                    problems left behind!

Gimmicks and Grace

Strange, isn't it Lord?

Those who are most eager to jump at any gimmick
        touted by media or medium
    as being "something for nothing"
Are sometimes the most reluctant to accept You at Your word
    that Your grace is a "free gift":
    The "something for nothing" offer of all time!

The Year of Our Lord

Jesus—
    How clearly we see you at
        Christmas-time,
        Cradled by Mary
        Protected by Joseph
        Worshipped by shepherds
        Honored by kings
    Enshrined on the altar
    And loved by the world.

But, oh Lord,
    Help us look for you, too,
        Among the taxes of life
        And the wanderings of rootless travellers
        In the world's smelly stables
        And in makeshift mangers
        In sweat-like drops of blood
        And rough-hewn crosses, humanly fashioned.
    Help us look, Lord—
        and help us find!

Not only at Christmas,
    But throughout a New Year that it might become indeed
    "The year of our Lord."

Lost and Found

Oh, God—how lost we are, we humans!

Surely it took more than just an apple,
a snake and a rebellious man and woman
To get us, our families,
our foreign policy and our environment
So lost in this maze of death and destruction,
Beyond the reach of reason, and
slipping from the grasp of sanity!

Centuries of rebellion,
20-megaton apples, and
the serpentine-myth of the "good life"
Have compounded the lostness.

But there's good news—
we're not yet beyond the reach of
the Babe in the manger
nor slipped from the grasp of a
nail-pierced hand!

Modern Miracle

Creator of the Body of Christ,

    Now, when freedom is god
           and "doing my own thing" the prevailing creed,
      when darkness is worshipped as light
        and discipline and commitment
           are dirty words,
    Empty pews are no surprise—
    The wonder is that the Church is alive!
This handful of the faithful,
       gathered to worship
          on this snowy, New Year's Sunday morn
—that, Lord, is the miracle!

Evangelism

I suspect, Savior,
    That salvation's not as simple
        as it's sometimes made to sound
        nor as quick as I wish it were;
    But rather the life-long discipline
        of letting Your Hand, Jesus Christ,
           put together the pieces
           of the puzzle of my life
           to reflect Your image when finished!

And You know, Master Puzzle-Maker,
    The more of me I let You assemble
    The more there is to proclaim
           to the puzzles around me,
"I know who can put you together, too!"

Divided Body

Lord Jesus—
    In Your earthly life, Your body was divided
        by tools of hatred
        —a spear
            some nails
                a thorny crown—
    and Your life flowed out upon the ground
        for each one of us.

What petty things we now allow
    to divide Your Body, the Church
    —how much to give to outreach,
        the pastor's beard,
            whether to buy drapes for the sanctuary.
And, as we pierce one another with unkind words,
    I can see Your life and love
        flowing out of us upon the ground—again!

Please, Lord,
    Don't let us crucify You again
        with our selfishness
            our stubbornness
            our bitterness
    For if we lose Your life
        we lose our own—now and forever.

Lord, save us from ourselves.

Rite of Passage

Most funerals depress me, Lord.
　　I know You are the Resurrection and the Life
　　I know there are many rooms in Your mansion
　　I'm eager to send a loved one from pain
　　　　　　to paradise—

But I'm troubled by the moisture on my cheeks!

Banks of beautiful flowers
　　piped in organ music of somber hymns
　　　　hours spent greeting weeping relatives
　　　　　　at the side of the open casket
Spread grief faster than the common cold!

But how cheap these tears seem
　　Considering that in this time
　　　　of handing our friend into Your care
　　We catch a glimpse of Your throne
　　　　the seat of all power
　　　　　　in heaven and on earth
　　　　　　in life and in death
　　　　and here we stand—
　　　　　　dressed only in the nakedness
　　　　　　　　of our mortality!

Now that is cause for tears—
　　tears of embarrassment for our delusions of
　　　　　　mortal grandeur
　　tears of frustration at our inability
　　　　　　to sit on that throne
　　and tears of humble gratitude that You are there
　　　　　　and love us!

Redeem us from our unrighteous rites, Oh Lord,
　　that we might weep with You,
　　　　　　not at You!

Easter Miracles

Is the greatest miracle of Easter
    really the Resurrection?
    Any god worth his salt
        would like to pull off a job like that
        if he could!
Or is it the Incarnation—
    the choosing to live, to suffer
        and to die among us
        and for us!
Only a God of Great Love would do that
    and You are that God
    and You did it!

Your rising gives us hope—
    but Your living gives us meaning now
    and Your dying—deliverance from ourselves!

As spring miracles of sun and rain green the sod
May these miracles of Easter green our souls
    with new life!

Spiritual Immunity

Lord Christ—

How it must grieve you!

Your Body, the Church,
 entrusted with the calling
 of "infecting" people with
 the "disease" of Jesus Christ
Succeeds so often instead—
 by frequent exposure to
  small, dead doses of
   churchly decorum
   and self-righteousness—
To build up resistance
  and
Only immunize the faithful
 against catching a good strong
  case of You!

Meeting of the Bored

Surely, Lord—
>   If You are in the midst of two
>   or three meeting together,
>   You must be among this twenty-five plus.
>   If You bless the cup of cold water
>   given in Your name
>   Plane-loads of blankets, food and
>   medicines must be warmed by Your
>   approval.

Ah, but Lord—
>   Finding You. There's the problem.

>   Catching a glimpse of Your will
>   admist the agenda at this time of night
>   Is like searching a puzzle for
>   secret figures hidden there.
>   Searching the obvious complexities
>   for the hidden order which helps
>   it all make sense.

But, oh!—
>   The joy of finding!

Praise, You, Lord, for revealing Yourself to us,
But thank You more for making us work hard
>   at finding You!

Church Conference

Now I know what St. Paul meant
    by being "surrounded by so great a
        cloud of witnesses."
Thousands of persons whose
    praying
        singing
            debating and
                loving
    have helped mold the lives of
        my great-grandparents
          my grandparents
            and my parents
    and now influence me
                    and my children.

With such a perspective and responsiblity
            as this
    no wonder the Church moves slowly
           in the face of change.

But we—we are to *"run* the race set
             before us"
    and what a tension results.

Foundation of the Church and
    Time-Keeper of our Race—
        Redeem our tension from conflict
      to creativity!

Ritual or Reality?

Great Hearer of Prayers and Seeker of Hearts—
  The pastor's wife is asked to pray publicly
   at so many traditional times
   and in so many proper places
  And I've done it dozens of times,
   in meaningful phrases.
 BUT, wrapped up in this ritual,
  I've neglected to come to You alone—
   stammering in my weakness
   spiritually naked in my need—
  and, suddenly, You seem so very far away!

  Like trying to build a marriage only
   on sermons about love,
    Form isn't foundation enough for faith,
     either!

  Forgive me my powerful pretensions,
   Come close to me again,
   and redeem my walk with You
    from ritual to reality!

Ruts and Redemption

Oh God of Constancy and Change,
      Ruts are so restful,
      Narrowness so nice
      and a closed mind so comfortable
That it takes mental dynamite
      to blast us loose
      from the familiar!
And how painful that is!

But that suffering saves us
      from the painless but certain death
            of suffocation,
      as our ruts grow to enclose us
            and shut out Your breath!

Redeem us from our ruts
      with Your heavenly high explosive
            —the Holy Spirit!